At the Construction Site

STEVEN JAMES PETRUCCIO

DOVER PUBLICATIONS, INC.
Mineola, New York

Note

In this book, you will see many workers on the job at a construction site. A construction site is a place where a new building goes up. It can be big or small, such as a tall office or a small house. Construction workers at the site use many types of trucks to do the job: these trucks dig up the ground and move dirt, break rocks, lift wood and steel parts to workers above the ground, and many other tasks. Look carefully at the pictures, and you will see that all of the workers at the site wear a "hard hat." Everyone at a construction site—even visitors—must wear this metal helmet-like hat to protect his or her head.

As you read about the jobs that the construction workers do, as well as the trucks that they use, you can enjoy coloring in the pictures. Have fun!

Bibliographical Note

At the Construction Site is a new work, first published by Dover Publications, Inc., in 2004.

International Standard Book Number

ISBN-13: 978-0-486-43661-6
ISBN-10: 0-486-43661-6

Manufactured in the United States by LSC Communications
43661607   2017
www.doverpublications.com

Work begins early in the morning at this
construction, or building, site.

These workers will help to put up a new building at the site.

This slow-moving truck had to be brought
to the site by another truck!

One truck is loading dirt into a dump truck, which will carry it away. A worker is breaking the ground with a jackhammer.

4

These two trucks use different machines to dig. The truck at
the bottom moves on a track, not wheels.

This truck driver uses a wrecking ball
to get rid of an old building.

A bulldozer is the right truck to use to clear the land.

A powerful digging truck can break through rock.
The driver moves controls to do the job.

Not all construction trucks are big. The small truck at the bottom is an "earth mover."

The front-end loader scoops up dirt and rocks.

The bucket is emptied into the back of a waiting dump truck.

The scraper truck makes the ground even so that the
building will be on flat ground.

Things needed to construct the building are
brought to the site.

A "clamshell" bucket easily digs a hole in the ground.

This crane crawls on a track that goes around and around.
The crane lowers pipes into the ground.

The dump truck fills up holes with dirt
from other parts of the site.

This line of dump trucks will carry dirt and rocks
away from the site.

This truck driver digs deep holes in the ground with
a heavy drill-like tool.

A "drop hammer" pounds a part of the new
building into the ground.

One worker builds a frame for the building,
while another digs up the ground.

A mixer pours concrete into the wood frame to make
the new building strong.

The driver uses a tall crane to lift a piece of steel in the air.
He will lower it carefully onto another piece of steel.

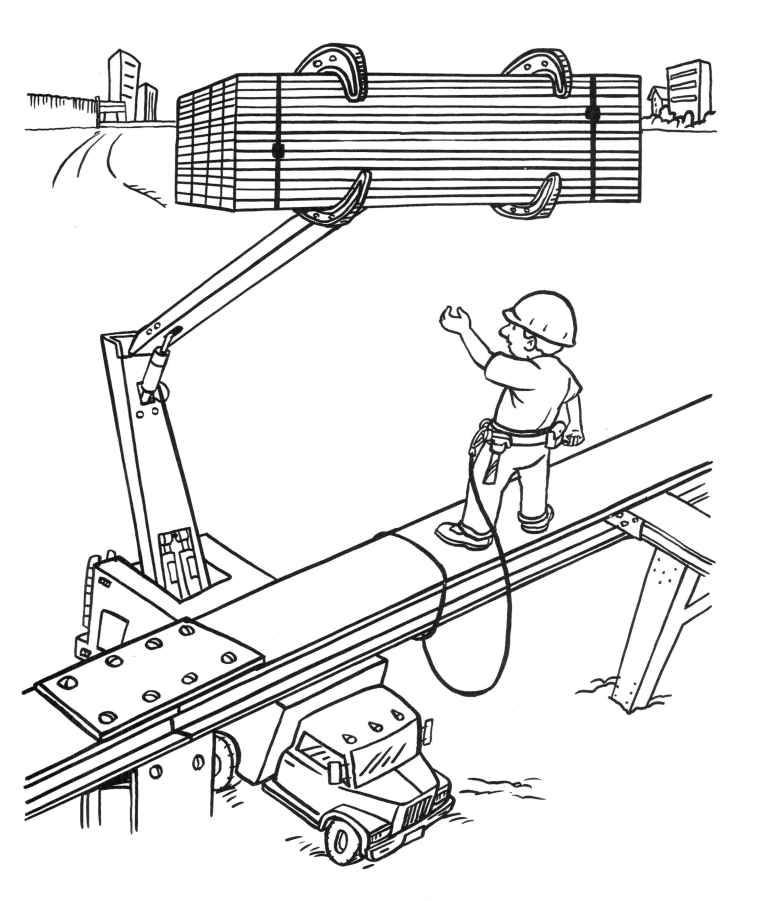

A "grappler" lifts slabs of concrete and takes them to a
worker high above the ground.

Workers build a "tower" crane at the site to lift concrete slabs to the workers.

This truck is called a "grader." It makes the ground smooth for a new road to be built.

A dump truck (at the top) leaves behind part of its load as it slowly moves along the new road.

Two workers ride on the back of the paver. A steamroller
flattens out the top of the new road.

This truck is called a cherry picker. A worker can ride in the
bucket at the top of the truck.

A tiny truck called a "mini loader" carries two trees to their new home at the site.

After much hard work, the new building finally is finished! The construction workers are proud of the job they have done.